For

~

D1325469

A MOTHER IS A SPECIAL PERSON

By Lois L. Kaufman

Illustrated by Richard Judson Zolan

PETER PAUPER PRESS, INC.
WHITE PLAINS, NEW YORK

*In loving memory of my mother,
who was a* very *special person*

∼

Artist: Richard Judson Zolan
Illustrations copyright ©1998
Art Licensing Properties, LLC.

Book design by Mullen & Katz

Introduction

*T*he most complex and finely detailed job description would probably not be sufficient to describe exactly what a mother does for her child. And even if this job description came close to listing a large portion of a mother's duties, it is unlikely that it would illuminate the care and love that a mother brings to these tasks.

A mother nourishes and counsels, helps heal wounds, and encourages dreams. She is a caregiver and confidante, a mathematician and a nutritionist, a chauffeur and a tutor. A mother's willingness to help her child reach his or her full potential is not exactly unsung, but it is likely that a mother does not hear often enough that her child is appreciative of all that she does. Sometimes simplicity conveys the message most clearly, and so, within the beautifully illustrated pages of this Keepsake of admiration and affection, the one theme that emerges clearly and continuously is that *you, Mother, are a special person.*

L. L. K.

A Mother is a Special Person

———— ≈ ————

*H*ow often tears are dried
by a mother's kiss. All injuries—
those you can see and those you
can't—disappear.

≈

*N*o matter how busy
a mother is, she always has time
for her children.

A Mother is a Special Person

As a daughter grows older,
her mother sometimes seems to
grow younger, until they're more
like sisters or friends.

~

*M*others and daughters
cooking together produce
good food and even
better memories.

A little girl
trying to walk in
Mom's high heels
will be wearing her own
only too soon.

A Mother is a Special Person

A mother's love
is unconditional.

*M*other's chicken soup warms
both the body and the soul.

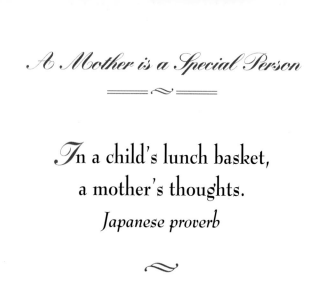

A Mother is a Special Person

*In a child's lunch basket,
a mother's thoughts.*

Japanese proverb

*Mothers reject the idea
that one could fail, and provide
the confidence to succeed.*

Childish messages
on a mother's
refrigerator door
could fill a
book of love.

A Mother is a Special Person

Petals of a flower may fade,
but a mother's love
blooms forever.

When a daughter sees herself
reflected in her mother's eyes, the
image is always beautiful.

A Mother is a Special Person

All mothers are rich when they
love their children.

There are no poor mothers,
no ugly ones, no old ones.

Their love is always the most
beautiful of the joys.

A Mother is a Special Person

And when they seem most sad, it
needs but a kiss which
they receive or give to turn all
their tears into stars in the depth
of their eyes.

Maurice Maeterlinck

A Mother is a Special Person

A mother's lullaby is
always sung in tune.

*S*haring and caring—
motherhood.

A Mother is a Special Person

A mother's arms are made
for hugging; her heart is
made for loving.

A child's first and best
schoolroom is her
mother's heart.

There is
no key to a
mother's heart.
It is always
unlocked.

A Mother is a Special Person

Mother is the one
who teaches you the meaning of
"Home is where the heart is."

A mother never outgrows
her role in life, no matter how
old her children are.

A Mother is a Special Person

May the moon watch over you
by night and the sun shine upon
you by day. This is
a mother's prayer.

A child does not have to
be taught how to love—it flows
naturally from its mother.

When we say
someone has been
"like a mother to me,"
it is the
ultimate compliment.

A Mother is a Special Person

"You were right" are words
to warm a mother's soul.

A woman's appreciation
of her mother deepens with
the birth of her own child.

A Mother is a Special Person

Who can find a virtuous woman?
for her price is far above rubies.

The heart of her husband doth safely
trust in her, so that he shall
have no need of spoil.

She will do him good and not evil
all the days of her life.

She stretcheth out her hand to the
poor; yea, she reacheth forth
her hands to the needy.

Strength and honor are her clothing;
and she shall rejoice in time to come.

A Mother is a Special Person

———— ~ ————

She openeth her mouth with wisdom;
and in her tongue is the law
of kindness.

She looketh well to the ways of her
household, and eateth not the bread
of idleness.

Her children arise up, and call her
blessed; her husband also,
and he praiseth her.

Proverbs 31:10-12, 20, 25-28

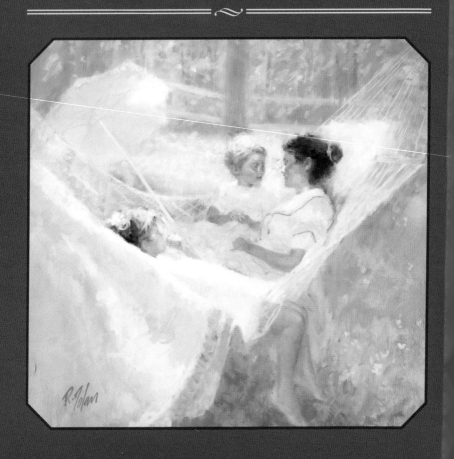

A Mother is a Special Person

There was a place in childhood,
that I remember well,

And there a voice of sweetest tone,
bright fairy tales did tell,

And gentle words, and fond embrace,
were given with joy to me,

When I was in that happy place upon
my mother's knee.

Samuel Lover

A Mother is a Special Person

―~―

*M*y mother had a slender, small body, but a large heart—a heart so large that everybody's grief and everybody's joys found welcome in it, and hospitable accommodation. The greatest difference which I find between her and the rest of the people whom I have known, is this, and it is a remarkable one: those others felt a strong interest in a few things, whereas to the very day of

her death, she felt a strong interest in the whole world and everything and everybody in it. In all her life she never knew such a thing as a half-hearted interest in affairs and people, or an interest which drew a line and left out certain affairs and was indifferent to certain people. The invalid who takes a strenuous and indestructible interest in every-thing and everybody but himself, and to whom a dull moment is an unknown thing and an impossibility, is a formidable adversary for disease and a hard invalid to vanquish. I am certain that it was this feature of my mother's makeup that carried her as far toward ninety . . . a mighty age, a well-contested fight for life for one who at forty was so delicate of body as to be accounted a confirmed invalid and destined to pass soon away. . . . Her interest in people and animals was warm, personal, friendly. She always found something to excuse, and as a rule to love, in the toughest of them— even if she had to put it there herself. She was the natural ally and friend of the friendless.

Mark Twain

A Mother is a Special Person

We never know the love of the parent till we become parents ourselves. When we first bend over the cradle of our own child, God throws back the temple door, and reveals to us the sacredness and mystery of the father's and mother's love to ourselves. And in later years, when they have gone from us, there is always a certain sorrow, that we cannot tell them we have found it out. One of the deepest experiences of a noble nature in reference to the loved ones that have passed beyond this world is the thought of what he might have been to them if he had known while they were living, what he has learned since they died.

Henry Ward Beecher

A Mother is a Special Person

A time comes
when you have to explain
to your children
why they were born,
and it's marvelous
if you know the reason
by then.
Hazel Scott